HabitLand

The Entry. The Residency. The EXODUS!

George "Coach G" Morning II

Self-n-DAYS
Publish 30   This Is The Year For
Your New Book

www.selfpublishn30days.com

Printed in the United States of America

ISBN: 978-1719217958

1. Habits 2. Empowerment

George Morning II: NGM NOW Enterprises, LLC

HabitLand

Disclaimer/Warning:

FOREWORD BY CRAIG PERRA

When I first met George, the author of this book, he was addicted to pornography and prescription medication, homeless, separated from his wife and children, and crashing on his mother's couch. He called me looking for help with his addiction and slew of other life problems (this was before I appeared on The Katie Couric and Steve Harvey Shows, with clients in 20 countries, so it was easy to track me down). He was low, he was down, and he was depressed. I talk to a lot of people who are low, but this call was special, and I'll never forget it. There was something about him that immediately resonated with me.

This was a man at his lowest yet the most important memory that I have of that first call is, "Holy s*** this guy is powerful." I just knew that this man, as broken as he was, had a gift. I could feel it buzzing through the phone. There was this fire-driven passion in his voice that struck me - I said to myself damn I wish I had that. He had this preacher vibe that I just loved and frankly I was a little envious. I just knew in my heart that George was going to change lives.

So I coached George, and he kicked serious ass. He did everything I asked and then some - he always had his own way of seeing things. I remember once during a coaching call he said something powerful and I wrote this deeply profound wisdom in my notebook to share with clients later. It was during this time that George became obsessed with habits. He so deeply wanted to escape from HabitLand - this place he lived for so long where he was a slave to the shitty habits that consumed him. He even asked me to train him as a professional life coach, and the rest is history.

The day he graduated from my Coach Training Program, his company shut down his office. That's when I knew divine intervention was at play. This was a man destined to empower others. I knew it, and the universe knew it too. He had a choice to make. Look for another job or start building his life coaching practice. He clearly made the right choice, and thousands are better because of it.

I'm honored to call George one of my proudest success stories. He's not just a friend, he's family. And what do you need to do at this very moment, dear reader? Right now, all you have to do is turn the page, because this book contains powerful tools that will help you break free from HabitLand so that you can embrace your power of choice. This book will change you. Keep reading.

DEDICATION

To the true escape-artists of HabitLand before I even knew it existed,

My Mother & Father: Deborah Threats and George I. Morning.

My Coaches and Mentors: Victor Bell, Craig Perra and Brian Thomas.

*And to my children & constant reminders to keep fighting
for my Exodus from HabitLand:*

Zion, Izayah, and Izabella.

TABLE OF CONTENTS

INTRODUCTION

"I HATE my life!"

"I'm just like my daddy."

"How can I be addicted to that?"

"I perform better than most, so my business is OK."

"Why can't I just STOP?"

"Boys will be boys…"

"I pay the bills, so don't question what I do!"

"It's not THAT bad what I do."

"Don't you see what you're doing to us?"

I've already FAILED once before, and I'll fail again…"

"I can't handle ALL of this in my life!"

"HOLY SHIT HOW DID I GET HERE?"

On that damn couch, in the midst of my own "HOLY SHIT" moment, all of these statements and more either ran through my head or was asked of me when I suffered with my addictions and failures. If you've found yourself in similar situations, odds are you've probably racked your brain for answers, searched high and low to just came away feeling even more lost and confused than ever!

It's like trying to get information to relate to the fish in water or the stars in space. You can learn everything about their environment, but without experiencing it, you're stuck with what basically amounts to a guess. An educated one, but still a guess! And that's what I was doing. Guessing. Refusing to listen or even hear others who were trying give me help; until I found myself on that fucking couch!

So what's the couch? Interestingly enough, it can look different for each of us. For me, it was where I found myself in the summer of 2013. On a literal couch in my momma's house riddled with shame and guilt. I was powerless. No sense of my identity. Homeless. An "unforgivable" sinner. A poor excuse for a husband. I was thought of as a monster by my two youngest children, and I was a witness to my oldest son copying my worst habits. I was completely unaware of what was really happening around me. I was stuck living this automatic, hazy, free fall life of addictions, coupled with a victim mindset designed to fulfill my ego, validate my experiences, and fuel my emotions.

For you it may look different. It might be in how you handle finances; spending beyond means, convinced you'll follow your budget next time around or the new account "will" happen or the new job "will" come thru, just to blame the job or account when the accounts are overdrawn. It might be the child with all the talent in the world scared to pursue their goals because they experienced failure before and blame life, peers, and lack support in the process. Or settling in performance expectations, to only wonder why a higher profit wasn't made or goal achieved. Or maybe it is as simple as yelling to get your point across or letting yourself get bullied in school, workplace or the damn grocery store. It's all the couch. And more defined, it's all HabitLand. And it's a place you need to LEAVE!

As you've probably already realized, I CUSS! When I experienced everything you're about to read, it didn't all happen in a well-spoken and polite place. And I doubt your fight with addiction, loss of family, company failure, or dream unrealized didn't feel like a pillow-fight. The conversations I had with myself weren't polite, nor were the conversations I had with my coaches. But they got the job done! For those who have truly lost what they most value, love, and desire, they didn't want politeness. They want RESULTS!

In the pages that follow, I'll take you through my entry, residency and Exodus of HabitLand. You'll learn about habits and addictions; what drives them; and, the tools you'll need to change them. For the addicts (and as a former addict), I know the road to recovery and help usually begins with either discovery, disclosure or exposure. However for most addicts, there is no disclosure - or willfully and openly confessing. We were caught! Discovered and EXPOSED! And what's stopping you from full recovery is the shame from it. And if we're being honest, there is no "disclosure". If you have already transparently told others you'd probably be further along by now.

Lastly, as much as I wrote this book to help the addicts around us, I'm also writing to fathers, husbands and business men. I need you all to avoid the losses I made before it costs you your family, finances and maybe even your faith.

PART I

ENTRY

*Let's get started! Part 1 gets us the nuts and bolts.
We are going to cover 3 important topics to get you
prepared for the following:*

- "What is a Habit?";
- The Habit Cycle; and,
- WELCOME TO HABITLAND

*Take a pen, highlighter and whatever you need to take notes.
Trust me. You'll want to!*

WHAT IS
A HABIT?

Ok. Let's get the easy stuff out the way and discuss habits. After all, I'm sure you didn't get a book called Habitland and expect to NOT learn about HABITS! So what is a habit? Most people and organizations believe that a habit is merely about consistent action over a period of time. I remember when I was in sales it was "Do this for 90 days and you'll have the habit." I would "quit" smoking or one of my addictions for weeks at a time just to go back. And we all know of people who quit the gym after 30 days or who quit a position or job after a few months. They never really developed the habit. So let's demystify this some!

THE DEFINITION

A habit is <u>an automatic response to an external trigger</u>. Think about that for a minute. All habits we have are nothing more than a product of our response to an external trigger. The alarm clock, the look of a woman as she walks, the scream of a hungry newborn, receiving a text from your spouse. All external and all "trigger" some type of response from us.

THE CYCLE

After knowing the the definition, it's important to know the habit cycle. In his best-selling book, "The Power of Habit," author Charles Duhigg explains a simple three-step process that all habits follow. This habit cycle from Duhigg is a 3 step cycle that's known as The Habit Loop; and says that each habit consists of...

1. The Cue: the event that starts the habit.
2. The Routine: the behavior that you perform, the habit itself.
3. The Reward: the benefit that is associated with the behavior.

And it looks a lot like this:

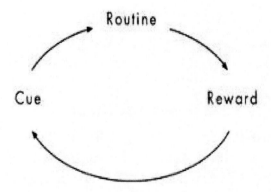

THE CYCLE V2.0

My man Charles created a useful 3 step cycle; however, it's missing 2 essential parts: THOUGHT and CRAVINGS/UNMET NEEDS! So let's upgrade the habit cycle to have a complete understanding. Here's the new habit cycle:

We got some new parts so let's take a minute and know what we're working with:

STEP 1: TRIGGER

Triggers are interesting. They may look a little different, but much like the gun part of the same name they are designed to do the same thing... START THE BANG! You'll recognize it as that instantaneous energy shift in your body when something happens. Whether it's the goosebumps from a surprise, the flash of heat when you're angered, or the elation from a loving message from your partner - it's all triggers.

Triggers are also biologically hard-wired to us! That's right! Our triggers are OUR triggers. It's why things will piss you off and not the friend next to you. And regardless of how bad or good the triggers are, they never go away! You can learn to gain greater control over them, but they will never go away!

Attacking the triggers for habit change is where people lose the fight in habit change. Change jobs. Different city. Trade old friends or new friends. You might get by with a temporary shift or change, but you can't outrun your triggers! Lastly, and most importantly, nobody cares. Seriously. If someone does something that triggers you, they more than likely won't stop.

STEP 2: THOUGHTS

Reasoning Power. A Developed Intention or Plan. THOUGHTS! So for good reason, this section is going to have a bit more meat on it. Your thoughts are just that important! As powerful as the craving/unmet need is to drive the habit cycle, the thought carry the same energy to drive our actions!

The problem with our thoughts is that most of us rely on our primal instincts that I like to call the Triple Es: Ego, Experiences and Emotions. For HabitLanders, the Triple Es lead directly to a range of thoughts that keep them in HabitLand and produce the actions of addicts and other compulsive behaviors. First up, we break down the Triple Es and then the 4 DEADLY THOUGHTS!

EGO

Don't freak out. Most men reading this are like "NOOOOOO! I need my ego!" And we do, to an extent. As vast as your ego will allow you to dream of your greatness, it won't allow for the level of humility and mindfulness needed to learn what you need to acquire your greatness. Even if you do not have an addiction, consider this quote from Wynton Marsalis, famous jazz musician, in a letter to an admirer admonishing him on the value of mindful humility:

Humility has nothing to do with me, your friends, your lady; and it's in such short supply out here, man. Do you know how you can tell when someone is truly humble? I believe there is one simple test: because they consistently observe and listen, the humble improve. They don't assume, "I know the way."

There is a constant battle within each of us to keep our egos in check from reaching too high or too low. Unchecked it oozes arrogance and demands to be entitled above all. If the slightest interest isn't present, your ego will not let you participate. Huge ego and a problem at work? More than likely you weren't productive. Huge ego and problems with your spouse? You're more likely to not even engage him or her until they do something to interest you. Our egos will cause us to miss countless opportunities simply because it doesn't create an immediate interest. If you are following your ego, then you're ALWAYS right, and being right just doesn't always get the job done!

I remember when I started sales, I NEEDED to know everything before I began anything! Afterall, I was a 30 yr. old college graduate in a room full of high school graduates. I wore a button down shirt and dress pants and had a resume of over a decade of experience, while my counterparts were dressed in t-shirts and shorts with little to no experience! And my manager was younger than me! From the first day all I did was argue what I thought was "right" daily.

"I need to know how to do ... before I start."

"Why do I get paid by ONLY commission?"

"This would work better if we did..."

Finally my manager sat me down and told me, "George, you've spent the week trying to convince me you're right and haven't made a sale. You can either fight to be right or make money and feed your family. What's it gonna be?" Needless to say from that point forward I was one of the best producers month in and month out!

EXPERIENCES

Think back to your childhood. Think about how you ate. How you dressed. How you spoke. How much of that exists today? For most of us very little, yet it amazes me how much other information from our past we allow to applicable to our lifestyle today! For most of us, our history damages our future more than fortifying it! What was right for us at 8 doesn't work at 18. And what we thought or knew at 18 has more than likely changed or at the very least shifted to some degree that no longer allows the same thinking.

The problem with our experiences, is that when we are not mindful in reviewing them, we align our thinking and motives with either the most positive or negative experiences of our past.

"I had a bad relationship in my past so I'll never trust again."
"My last girlfriend cheated on me so I'm done with relationships."
"My dad left when I was a child so I know all men leave one day."

"Oh my God! I had the best date ever! He SAID he's ready to change for
GOOD as soon as we're back together!"
"School's a breeze. I got by in high school barely studying and I'll do the
same in college... TOO EASY!"

I'm a huge fan of Outback Steakhouse and for a while considered their steak to be the BEST... until I went to Morton's! I thought I had died and gone to heaven! And then there's this steak house in NY that I can't remember the name of but can find it in my sleep! My point is that I was CERTAIN that Outback was the best. I had great "experiences" there with the steak. But if I let that be the guide then... no REALLY great steak at some spot in NY! Does it mean that Outback doesn't have a good steak? No. It doesn't mean it's the best either, at least not for me.

Here's the deal. There is value in all of your experiences. But if you don't apply the education learned, then the value is lost. Our experiences are only as valuable as the lesson we learn from them. Losing one fight doesn't mean losing every fight. Being a product of two generations of divorced and addicted men doesn't mean that's the outcome for me and my children.

Really think you can get away with what worked at the lower level on the next level? Then why are more men dropping out of college today then 10 years ago? Furthermore, if you just "got by" before, how much longer do you want that existence? Don't let your past experiences navigate your future. Use or gain the education to override your experiences!

EMOTIONS

Do you still have temper tantrums? Like full blown kicking and punching the ground? Probably not if you're an adult. You learned that it really got you nowhere. Like that time you got in a fight, just for someone to make you sit down and work it out? As you grew you experienced other emotions. Most of us aren't with our first love. Most of us aren't very close to our elementary classmates.

The problem with emotions is that they're subjective, not objective. If you've had a shitty life, or maybe you've been so jaded by your past that you are numb to pain and hurt. It's why I stayed high or acted out! I wanted that numbness. I wanted to not "feel" the pressure of the day or of my life. And when I wasn't, my emotions were volatile and unpredictable. I couldn't trust them.

The Triple E's are how we have learned since infancy! But it cannot be the only way we learn and interact with the world and those involved in it. Specifically, if you live or operate with a victim's mindset, your first thoughts filled with emotions, ego, and experiences will manifest directly into the Four Deadly Thoughts!

FOUR DEADLY THOUGHTS

So let's break down those "deadly thoughts" I mentioned before. Amongst all the traits and characteristics above, you need to understand that when you become as a HabitLander, you are a SLAVE to your triggers and the thoughts that follow! Here's what I learned: there are essentially four deadly thoughts that for the most part guide our actions while in HabitLand. Let's talk about them.

DEADLY THOUGHT #1:
SELF-DEPRECATING THOUGHTS

"I'm a LOSER!" "My life SUCKS!" "I'm such a piece of SHIT!"
"I should have never started this!"

Do you recognize these statements? Do they sound familiar? These are examples of self-deprecating thoughts, and these statements and many more like them ran through my mind always. Self-Deprecating thoughts were always telling me how crappy I was, how glass was always half empty, or I could never do "good enough." It didn't matter if it was as simple as forgetting to take out the trash or something major like relapsing after I swore off my addictions. These thoughts came to the surface so damn FAST! We normally hear these thoughts when areas of shame and guilt arise when we are questioned or held accountable.

DEADLY THOUGHT #2:
SELF-DOUBT THOUGHTS

"I can't." "I'm unable to..." "I'll never..."

Almost as dangerous as self-deprecating thoughts, these thoughts defeat us BEFORE we ever get started and they rarely let us even begin the process of getting better! These were the ones that kept me on the couch. If I failed before, I'd fail again. I remember in the first few coaching sessions I had with my coach and now mentor and friend, Craig Perra, founder of The Mindful Habit, I had self-doubt thoughts running CRAZY! "I'll never get rid of this habit." "I can't stop drinking, buying drugs, watching porn or change my life for the better!"

DEADLY THOUGHT #3:
SELF-ENTITLEMENT THOUGHTS

"I deserve to..." "If you didn't ... then I wouldn't..."

These are the thoughts we LIKE!!!! Self-Entitlement thoughts permit us to do the unhealthy actions and remove the accountability from us! Make no mistake, we are entitled to something... THE PURSUIT OF A GREAT LIFE!!! We are not entitled to an unhealthy lifestyle of any type, and unfortunately, these thoughts if left unchecked can do just that!

Think about a diet. You kept a GREAT diet all month long. And then that one day happens where you start to hear yourself say, *"I deserve..."* something unhealthy -- a day from the gym, ice cream, candy, etc., and ultimately unproductive! Or that last outfit or pair of shoes you just "had" to have! Maybe you feel wronged by someone, like that driver who cut you off! As you're yelling and flicking him the bird as you drive by, the thought is something like, *"It's YOUR FAULT I did ..."*.

Lol. I would make up tons of excuses for things like eating out when I was at work while my family was home eating whatever was in the fridge. Of course I was damaging the budget and finances. But the only thoughts I had were "I work all day... I deserve to have a meal if I want it!" or "If you made my lunch before I left for work..." Did I feel justified at the moment? Yeah. Did it make my actions any more right? Nope. Not one time did it make my actions right because I somehow felt entitled to do the wrong thing.

Even in education, I see it with the youth. Hearing kids curse out loud, verbally and/or physically attack another student or staff member, just for the offender to say, "I know I was wrong, but she/he did/said…" as if what was said somehow equated to the offense committed.

DEADLY THOUGHT #4:
PERSONAL OBJECTIFYING THOUGHTS

"Look at her ass!" "If I had this house I'd…" "Why does he have that position?" "Why can't my husband/wife act like that?"

As a recovering addict, I more commonly know these thoughts as my sexual or "high" thoughts. These were, of course, the more obvious, easily recognizable ones. However, I want to present the areas that require the most work: the objectifying of not only a person, but property and ideas!

Objectifying happens within moments. What starts as a gaze becomes a thought of possession and ownership. This thought makes us view people as objects and objects as greater value than presented.

Maybe you've seen a friend in a position you desired or coworker or a passerby or with your favorite car in a position you desired. It's one thing to want the position or a particular item, it's another thing to desire someone else's life and think you could operate it better.

THOUGHTS REVIEW

There was a lot to unpack with the thoughts! Before we proceed, we need to understand and be aware of one distinct trait of your thoughts. I gave you a hint with the first three… SELF! That's right. Your thoughts, no matter how entitled, doubtful, deprecated or personified, they are your creation! It's easy to say, "You made me feel…" but no one can control YOUR THOUGHTS! YOU are responsible for YOUR THOUGHTS!

The irony about these thought patterns is that they don't discriminate! Addict or not. Young or old. Gay or straight. Professional or unemployed. Global companies or the corner store. Educated or uneducated. It doesn't matter. It's not a question of "IF" you or I have these thoughts, but if we are aware of what these thoughts look like within each of us. Master knowing and changing these thoughts, it will put you in the exact spot you need to be to change your habits and be free of HabitLand!

STEP 3: ACTION

Actions are the followers and physical manifestations of our thoughts; hence why we spent so much time on our thoughts. They are the outcome and product everyone sees. Whether it's going to the gym, stopping at the nearest fast food restaurant, lighting up or whatever, it's the action. The action is also what we are judged by. It's how we and others judge HabitLanders.

Unfortunately this is also where most who are trying to break their habits and addictions fail. You can't just try to stop or control the action *soley*. Trying to stop the action and not addressing the triggers, thoughts or cravings is a lot like chaining up your refrigerator and pantry to lose weight. While I can guarantee that you'll lose weight by day 3, I can also guarantee that by day 5 you'll break into your neighbor's house for food. Addressing the action ONLY is a short-lived solution!

STEP 4: CRAVING/UNMET NEEDS

More commonly referred to as unmet needs in psychology, the term refers to the needs that a person didn't manage to satisfy yet. Just like there are physical needs such as the need to eat or the need to sleep, there are psychological needs that people must fulfill in order to feel good.

When people fail to satisfy their important unmet needs, they become depressed, and when people manage to fulfill their unmet needs, they experience true happiness. Unmet needs might also result in unhealthy addictions. Many of the substance abusers and many of those who are addicted to bad habits are just trying to satisfy an important unmet need that they didn't manage to satisfy otherwise.

Ok. Remember that time you was STARVING! You wanted a home-cooked meal with all of the fixings, but settled for that drive-thru, and still don't feel quite satisfied? Or even that time when you did something completely out of character, for one reason, just to regret it later? That's cravings and this is also where a significant amount of work goes with my clients.

I speak to many men who say, "I don't think I have a problem." Which is fine. Alcohol, gambling, and porn industries are multi-billion dollar industries for a reason. There are people who watch and perform porn; drink daily; gamble their life away all without any feelings of shame and guilt AFTER the action. But then there are those like us, who feel nothing but shame and guilt. If that's you, then cravings aren't met and habits need to be changed!

Remember, our habits are driven by our cravings. Repeat it! "YOUR HABITS ARE DRIVEN BY YOUR CRAVINGS!" <u>Not how long you do it. Not with a certain plan or system. If you don't crave it, your habits won't last, nor will you know how to break them!</u>

Let's make this applicable. If you've ever smoked, was the craving to smell like smoke, alienate yourself, chew a dozen mints, and/or become at risk for various life-threatening diseases? No. Does the drug addict crave being untrustworthy, a criminal, someone pitied and feared by the most loved ones? No. Does the child who acts out in home or school want to be disciplined, upset those who encourage them daily, or be known as the "problem child?" No. They all in some degree wanted attention, growth, space, purpose, a way to desensitize, time to think, an escape, or something not even listed here! The consequences of our actions are secondary to the cravings!

5TH & FINAL STEP OF THE HABIT CYCLE

There's a 5th part of this habit cycle that we'll discuss later, but it's a game changer too!

WELCOME TO HABITLAND!!!!

So what's "HabitLand?" Before we really get into HabitLand, I want to make one point crystal clear – **HabitLand isn't about just the habit; it's about the habit, mindset, and purpose for which it is done.**

Most people envision HabitLand as the place for addicts and desolates. Not entirely true. In fact, scientists estimate that humans on average spend close to 40% - 50% of our day in HabitLand. And for good reason! We aren't relearning how to tie our shoes, or get dressed for work or bathe. For the better part, most of us can't remember every detail on our daily commute to work. We look up and were there!

HabitLand can have some great benefits. For one it's automatic. We need that. It makes life move faster! Do you know how long it would take you to walk through life if you had to do stuff like tying your shoes like it's the first time every time? Or watching your every step as you walk to the door? Or if we had to read a script every time the phone rings or you meet a new customer? We couldn't make it through life if we didn't go to HabitLand from time to time.

Secondly, you're numb to the elements of your life. Think about athletes who can block out the cold or pain they are suffering during a game, or the professional who blocks out the annoying co-worker or mean boss. Let's be honest; if we were subject to every emotional whim, we'd still be just as unproductive in life. Again, we do need HabitLand!

You're probably saying, "Well if it's so good, then why are we trying to leave?" Good question. Consider HabitLand like your favorite vacation spot! Maybe it's skiing on the soft, new snow of the Alps, Bora Bora, or a sunny beach with clear waters and sand as soft as powder. Great ain't it? Now picture going in the worst conditions! The Alps in a drought. Bora Bora or some beach during a tsunami or hurricane. Not so good huh? You're like "Nah G. No bueno. Not my idea of a vacation."

So am I saying HabitLand is bad? Not at all. However, I am saying that like any vacation, you need to know when to go, be sure you go for the right reasons, and most importantly, know how and when to leave!

Alright. Now that we got the easy stuff out of the way, let's dig more into HabitLand. Upon Entry, there are a few significant areas we need to be aware of: Identity and Choices! These two areas get hit the hardest upon entering into HabitLand, but also are the indicators you need to be mindful about!

IDENTITY

One of my favorite movies "Wanted", with James McAvoy and Angelina Jolie, has this scene when Angelina's character starts beating the shit out of James' character and asking him, "Who are you?" He gives a bunch of responses, to which earns another punch from her brass knuckles. After a brutal hit and being asked "Who Are YOU?" he finally replies, "I DON'T KNOW WHO I AM!" Most of us are right there. Life is hitting you with brass knuckles and you're unsure of who you are when it does. For HabitLanders, this question is answered through their Labels, Roles and Trends!

LABELS & ROLES

So real quick? Who are you? Was one of your first 3 responses a label or a role? Maybe dad, executive, parent? It's not wrong that we have labels or roles, but when we become the label or role. Labels and roles provide structure to a particular environment (work, home, social, spiritual, etc.), however they do not define you. When we find most men and women in HabitLand their day tends to revolve around the roles, not the true needs of the individual. A "normal" day in HabitLand for me was looked a lot like the following:

6am - 7am: Husband
7am - 8:30am: Dad
8:30am - 10pm: Salesman
10pm - 12am: Husband
12am - 3am: Addict

May sound bad but it was EASY! As a Habitlander, I lived for this! All we have to do is be the role. The roles are easy because we just have to aim to be slightly better than that, not a better version of ourselves!

COMMON TRENDS

In addition to the role and labels, in HabitLand you live around the *common trends*. You know what the common trends are. It's that company or organization that is happy with doing better than average in their industry, but not the *best* the company can do. It's the system that continues to operate without care for consequences because "it's how we've always done it!" Or if you aren't as bad as those around you, but still have the addiction or concern. Not too high, but high enough that you "appear" better than the common trends. You are masked by being slightly better than the trend yet make excuses for lack of production.

I viewed the common trends of black men and sought to be as best as I could above it. I had custody of my oldest child, graduated from college, never "arrested" (holding ain't quite jail lol), got married, and "appeared" better than my peers, family and predecessors for that matter. And what made it even better was that I had nothing more to do than adhere to the roles and labels I had acquired. Not my identity or who I was born, but what I became.

THE TAKEAWAY

Habits are difficult to understand, let alone make or break, especially when trying to understand how they work in and around our lives. But they are needed; and like most good things, they can be abused and manipulated to cause harm. So before we move into HabitLand, review the following takeaways from the habit cycle and definition that you can readily refer to!

WHAT IS A HABIT?

- Automatic reaction to an external stimuli

WHAT IS THE HABIT CYCLE?

Triggers

- Step 1 of the Habit Cycle
- They NEVER go away!
- We are biologically hardwired for them – what triggers you is only about you!
- No one cares about them. Seriously.
- HITS LIGHTNING FAST!

Thoughts

- Step 2 of the Habit Cycle
- HITS ALMOST AS FAST AS TRIGGERS!
- Only you know them
- Most people have 20-30+ years of "bad programming" from family, friends, peers and society that primarily dominate their thought patterns

- All thoughts are rooted in our Ego, Emotions and Experiences
- 4 Deadly Thoughts to be aware of!

Actions

- Step 3 of the Habit Cycle
- Product of our thoughts
- Symptoms of the cravings/unmet needs
- What the world sees and judges us on.

Cravings & Unmet Needs

- Step 4 of the Habit Cycle
- What we desire to satisfy.
- What most people seek to satisfy with finances or physical intimacy -- NOT REAL CRAVINGS!
- Engine of the Habit Cycle

WELCOME TO HABITLAND!

Identity based on:

- Common Trends
- Labels & Roles

PART II

RESIDENCY

It's pretty easy to take up residency in HabitLand.
It doesn't require Good or Bad credit, nor does it matter if you want to
rent or own. All HabitLand requires of its residents is a:

- ROCK SOLID Victim Mindset;
- 3 Specific Responses to Fear, Change and Crisis; and,
- 2 Big distractions to keep you... Well... DISTRACTED!

Short but good section!
Let's check out some new property in HabitLand!

VICTIM MINDSET

T o best illustrate this, let's talk SUPERHEROES! Aside from their abilities, gadgets and cool costumes; what are the differences between victims and heroes? Quite a few! One of the biggest is that victims need SAVING while heroes need HELP! Go back and look at your favorite superhero show, movie or comic book. From time to time every superhero needs some help. Superman is like one of the strongest characters out! He can fly in space, bullet-proof, heat and x-ray vision. But if he needs something done with the sea, he goes and finds Aquaman. If a particular bad guy keeps escaping the law and goes beyond his morals, he goes and finds Batman! Heroes need help.

Victims, on the other hand, are COMPLETELY different! They stay in the same situation by keeping the SAME ROUTINE of running from fear, hiding from the challenges or waiting for either the villain to stop wreaking havoc or for the superhero to come and "save the day". Now, here's where it gets really interesting for victims. They never left the city! You never read or saw how all the citizens started taking karate or self-defense courses. You never heard a superhero say, "The good people of this great city no longer need my SAVING! Victims never improve past the need for saving. Heroes seek help before the real crisis, victims need saving during the crisis. Again, victims need saving, heroes need help.

Even worse, victims find "joy" in the rubble. The aftermath of whatever destruction they witnessed, they find comfort there, as if it's almost harder to live without it. You know the type. They live for life in chaos! One bad relationship after another. One employment complaint after another. One family complaint after another. And endless cycle of living in blame without the "need" for change. The proverbial Mr. or Mrs. "Woe is ME".

Victims also hang out with other victims or mask themselves in crowds of villains and heroes. They need to. It's the beauty of Habit-Land. We either feel supported to dwell in blame mode or can forget ourselves and think we are something we're not by association. They can either keep blaming the bad guy for the crisis because it happened or find fault with the good guy for the blessing because it didn't happen soon enough. Or both!

We all have either been apart of that crowd or know of it. Where no one in the group changes. No growth. I was apart of that group. I was apart of the group of men who didn't seek to improve their marriage, yet pursued every opportunity for an affair. I was apart of that group that got high and drank all day and worried about work when the intoxicants ran low.

Lastly, victims rarely understand that you are *only* a victim at the moment. After that moment, we are no longer victims, we suffer the effects of being victimized. And the reason we hold onto victim is that there is this other-worldly, life-altering version of comfort with the victim mindset.

I want to be clear. I didn't say we or anyone for that matter *wants* to be victims. We all have experienced being a victims at some point in our lives. And unfortunately, there are some of us who believe that the gravity or severity of the victim event allows us to remain a victim that much longer. It's become a commonly accepted practice in our culture. We celebrate being a victim in order to provide validation, substantial reasoning as to the "why" of the victim event, but not for growth from, but acceptance of!

Other traits of a victim mindset I experienced and coached against with my clients were:

- Need for external motivation over internal mindset;

- Assimilating to the crowd instead of celebrating uniqueness;

- Lives based on FEAR opposed to TRUST;

- Blames others rather than take ownership;

- Emotionally-driven vs. a practitioner of Mindfulness;

- And so much more!

HabitLander experience all of them and more! I "convinced" myself that it was ok to blame my family, job, peers, the "white man," and anything or anyone else that allowed me to be unaccountable to my actions and behaviors. It allowed me to believe that if my addictions weren't exactly like those of my father that I was somehow better. It gave me the justification to accept the least of life -- the least me. The victim me.

3 RESPONSES TO FEAR, CHANGE, AND CRISIS

Victims also respond to fear, change, and crisis in very distinct ways. Grant Cardone, author and sales expert, wrote about similar responses in relation to how individuals and businesses respond to economic crisis in his book, <u>If You're Not First, You're Last.</u> And I see why! Let's be honest, an economic crisis can bring about fear, change, and crisis!

THE "CHEERLEADER" RESPONSE

Think about a football or basketball game. Aside from the crowd, what voice is the loudest? The cheerleaders! Good cheerleaders are awesome! No matter what the outcome is, they keep the same cheer! Losing or winning, it's the same damn cheer. As encouraging as they can be, how much of an effect do they have on the actual game? Don't get me wrong, we all need a pep talk from time to time. But IN the game, do the have as big of an impact as the players or coaches? NO! As cheerleaders they have the loudest voice, but have the least impact!

That's the cheerleader response! Loudest and least effective! The cheerleader response allows HabitLanders to believe that they are the only ones affected by the change, fear or crisis. They refuse to accept that a change has happened, and that talk, not action, is what is needed to address the change, fear or crisis!

So how did I show my cheerleader response? Well, I was the guy who would complain about the "unfairness" of being fired, and not seek the next job immediately. Or a change in my job changed how I performed my role (remember, HabitLanders love their roles!). I would hear my ex-wife complain about her unhappiness and my infidelity and would get into a shouting match with her about what she did or didn't do all to create this justification that was "loud" enough to drown out the change, fear, and crisis around me.

THE "OLD SCHOOL" RESPONSE

You ever look for a job, do poorly with managing your finances, or break up with your partner and you have that "I gotta get back to basics" moment? Here's the problem with that common type of thinking. NOTHING IS THE SAME AS WHEN YOU FIRST BEGAN! You see, this response, rooted in our experiences, implies that nothing has changed from the beginning of one event to the end of the same.

I would lose a job and go back to how I got it, sending out a boatload of resumes. Now, some of you are like "Exactly! That's what you're supposed to do! Get back to basics!" Wrong. You see, even though I sent out a boatload of resumes, the reason I got fired was for having poor work ethics, improper use of company computers, and couldn't get to work on time! So if I make the "Old School" response, I don't change any of those faults. I do the action with the same mindset. Getting the job was easy. Keeping it was the issue that was needed to be addressed!

So, should I have been surprised when I lost job after job for the same reason? No. But of course, I was. Just like for the life of me I couldn't understand why I could make more money, but end up just as broke while never changing my spending habits. Why I could see doctor after doctor in an effort to improve my health just to go back to the same habits that got me in the ER in the to get pills and drugs to feel better instead first place?

THE "QUITTER" RESPONSE

One of the things about having a victim mindset is that quitting is easy to do. It's even easy to disguise in how we respond to life events. Habit-Landers find it easier and easier to seek only the low-hanging fruit, or charity. Now there is ABSOLUTELY nothing wrong with taking charity when needed. Hell, I've needed it before and may need it again in some fashion in the future! However, if you're seeking low hanging fruit or charity because it's "easier" to only seek that and not strive for higher goals like I did, then you're just masking your quit with the least of your capacity. Lastly, they roll up in a ball or the fetal position and wait for it to end.

After suffering rejection or failure (at my hands), I'd seek the least of a position! I'd always talk of aspiring for more, speaking about my potential. However, the outcomes showed the pursuit of what was easy to get. It was asking my parents or wife or family to do what was possible for me to do and provide. I was that guy who would sign up for every free seminar, webinar, promotion or whatever I thought would give me the advantage without doing the work, and more importantly, not making the <u>investment</u>!

Personally, I was that guy who would hear my wife complain about my addictions and get the least amount of help. I would just get the free download or session and proclaim "I'M CURED!" If I owed money to my family or other debt or financial responsibilities, I'd pay the least, or ignore the calls! Any of this sound familiar?

CONSEQUENCES OF THE FIRST 3 RESPONSES

Before we discuss the ONE response to fear, change, and crisis that is productive for everyone, it's important to understand the #1 reason to avoid the first three responses. It's quite simple. Whether we are talking about finances or your personal choices, addictions, and responses to life events, the question is ultimately: Do you want to leave debt and regret or a legacy when you die?

Let that sink in a bit. Think about what a family has to do if they have debt to handle from a loved one. Do you think it's something spoken of at family reunions fondly? Do you think it's a practice your family would want to duplicate? "Hey, guys! Guess what! Dad left us $1,000,000... **IN DEBT**! Let's get together and talk about how we can do the same to our families! YAY!" No. Not at all. In fact, they would work to get rid of the debt. To get rid of the one thing you left them. They would essentially erase you. Your legacy ends! If you make the right response to life events, leave healthy examples, and finances, then you leave something to be remembered, valued, and duplicated. Now you get to leave a legacy!

DISTRACTIONS

So how do you keep yourself from thinking about your victim mindset? After all, HabitLanders don't want to be reminded of their victim mentality. So, we get lost in distractions! Man, I loved my distractions! It's like the drug of HabitLand. I got a buzz and all! You don't even see the carnage around you with distractions.

The two distractions I became unknowingly obsessed with have been around since the DAWN OF TIME!

FAMILY & SOCIAL MEDIA!

Ok. Maybe social media hasn't been since the dawn of time, but you get my drift. The primary distractions allow HabitLanders to reinvent themselves; be enabled or justified; or to escape the reality of what we live, even past being in HabitLand. The beauty of my distractions is that they each fulfilled some part of me that I hadn't quite figured how to fill any differently. We'll discuss that later, but these distractions on a lesser scale than my addictions somehow made me feel a sense of significance. Importance even.

DISTRACTION #1:

Social Media

I LOVED the creation of the internet! Like a kid going to college or a new neighborhood, I got to reinvent myself through social media! MySpace, FaceBook, online dating sites, you name it I was on it. I was fed images that contributed to a version of myself that I believed was somehow of greater importance than who I was. It was masking a man riddled with the guilt and shame of who I really was.

The bogus email subscriptions. The apps that I "needed" for blah blah blah. Joining every social media platform and group. "Friending" anyone I could be new with, not the real me. What's really cool for HabitLanders is that with social media, you can literally "post" about a non-existent or half-assed attempt at recovery or change and the world of that platform will congratulate you and stroke your ego without any real work being done!

Online I could be witty, smart, attractive, bold, and so much more! I was a helper and present friend. I convinced myself that I was desired, wanted, and appreciated. And, just as false as the images and versions of me I presented, so were the responses I received. But it didn't matter. All that mattered was that it did the job, even if falsely and temporarily. I wasn't a victim. Not in this new, digital, inventive world.

DISTRACTION #2:

Family, Friends and Peers

As a HabitLander, you'll more than likely find yourself in one of two roles with your family, friends and peers: you are either the one most concerned for or the one most sought after. And more often than not we want to be seen as the "savior", answer man or problem solver while I was lost in my own questions. Either way, Either way, I didn't feel like a victim.

How many times have you known of someone who would religiously rush to the rescue of another, when in reality they need saving also? When in reality they need saving? I either went to family at the last minute to get the rent paid or relished having the rent at the last moment, rather than saving from every check to handle the obligation. I'd run at a moment's notice to somehow "rescue" someone in one moment, or hide when I felt I was useless.

THE TAKEAWAY

Victim Mindset is very specific in behaviors and beliefs... and so are the responses to fear, change, and crisis that accompany it! Know the traits and the distractions that hide them!

Victim Mindset

- Mindset after the victim moment
- Needing saving vs. seeking help
- Attracted to each other
- Will stay in the chaos

3 Responses to Fear, Change & Crisis

- Cheerleader Response: A lot of talking with no action
- Old School Response: Using old solutions for new problems
- Quitters Response: Seeking the low-hanging fruit; unwilling to make an investment
- Consequences of the 3 Responses: Leaving your loved ones a debt vs. leaving them a LEGACY!

Distractions

- Family, Friends and Peers allow for recreation or enabling of self image
- Social Media provides hiding gound for those who are victims

PART III

EXODUS

It's breakout time! As you can imagine it's gonna take more work to get out than it was to get in Habitland, so let's get right to it. This will be the hardest transition and work required in this journey. It requires embracing the fear, change or crisis AND understanding that previous methods and circumstances needed to overcome have changed. Remember, HabitLand won't let you leave without a fight! Pack your escape bag with:

- Rock Bottom;
- Choices;
- Advance & Conquer Response;
- Healthy Selfish;
- Real Identity (not that BS we had back in Entry);
- Cravings;
- "Goals: The What, How & WHY!"; and
- 3 Kick Ass Tools!

Alright. No time like NOW! Let's get to the Exodus...

I HIT ROCK BOTTOM!

I don't care who you are or what you do, there is probably no better place for the best takeoff than ROCK BOTTOM! Can you make your Exodus out of HabitLand without hitting your rock bottom? Absolutely! And I hope you can. But for most we get here. Most, if not all, millionaires or billionaires were bankrupt and disgraced before reaching their wealth. It takes a drastic health concern to make a drastic change. And for some it may take you having your worst relationship before you actually know what you want in a relationship, and from yourself. So if we're here, let's find the value of it!

It was my first moment of clarity. For the first time in a long time I actually *wanted and needed* to make healthy choices for myself. I caught a horrifics glimpse of what the effects of my lifestyle had on those I loved and on myself – now and in the future. Most importantly, what I did wasn't for another. Family broken and gone. Career all but gone. It was the first time when I realized that the next step I took was going to be just about me. I needed to…

MAKE A DAMN CHOICE!

Every man builds his world in his own image; he has the power to choose,
but no power to escape the necessity of choice. If he abdicates his power,
he abdicates the status of man, and the grinding chaos of the irrational
is what he achieves as his sphere of existence – by his own choice."

~ Ayn Rand ~

Remember that 5th part of the habit cycle I discussed earlier? Well here it is… CHOICE! Your choice and ability to exert it exists before the trigger, between the trigger and thought, between thought and action AND AFTER THE ACTION! Whether you're an admitted addict or live the ideal life, we all have this… CHOICES!

As cliche as it sounds it's amazing how little we disregard the full strength of our choices! Spiritually it's the first great gift given to us by the Creator in the form of free will. For those who don't believe in a higher power, it's still the one thing you have sole possession over. No one can take it from you. And the most damaging thing about our entry into HabitLand is how it affects our choices.

To better understand choices, let's break them down into 3 parts that are more often overlooked by HabitLanders:

- Power;

- Potential; and,

- Work!

THE POWER

First and foremost, your choice is your power. If you can't make a choice, then you have NO *POWER*! We take for granted and underestimate this so much in our daily doings. We regard the choice to turn left or right with the same regard as to whether to cheat on our spouse or not. In HabitLand, the power of choice is more about immediate gratification rather than long term gratification and yet we wonder why we feel a loss of control.

For a moment think of the last time you said, "It's out of my control." or "I don't have a choice about..." Everytime those sentiments were echoed or thought of, it was nothing more than you not using your power of choice. There's always a choice. Even if the option or alternative seems insurmountable, it's 10 times better to say, "I choose to not do..." than to say "It's out of my control..." A simple equation I learned in sales works here as well "X = X = X". Each X is unknown, except for the first one. The only one you have any control over. Remember the following formula if you get nothing else out of this book:

CHOICE = POWER = CONTROL OF YOUR LIFE!

THE POTENTIAL

Secondly, In HabitLand, we have no comprehension of the *potential* of our choices. Aside from my addictions, I was NOTORIOUSLY bad with money! I wasn't check to check, I was check to Wednesday before payday! And it's not that I didn't make "good" money, but I never saw past the two week pay period ahead of me. I spent on myself, family, whatever else and never saw the full potential of my choice to splurge or to save. Short-term potential is all we see in HabitLand -- the benefit of "now" from our choices. The potential is only about what feels, looks, or tastes good now -- not the impact moments ahead, let alone years ahead.

In HabitLand that foresight goes out the window. We make choices based on emotions, ego and experiences and its those choices that leave us the most blindsided wondering how something happened or quoting "Why is something ALWAYS happening to me!" song.

Luckily I had a good friend who had no shame in pointing this out to me. After helping me for the uptenth time, a good friend of mine candidly told me, "Bro. I love you... BUT You gotta get your shit together. And that means you gotta get this car right. And THAT means you need to start looking 5 years ahead of you and say 'OK. what can happen?' cause the shit is gonna happen! And that includes the good shit you're going after. But if you continue to only plan for the good shit, you'll never get it 'cause the bad shit you ain't plan for WILL happen! It's GUARANTEED to happen and you need to fucking know that!"

After a moment of silence and me cussing him out in my head, I realized he was right. I only saw the short-sighted "right now" potential of my choices.

One donut. Does it lead to only satisfying your tastes buds or to diabetes, obesity and other health complications?

One kiss. Does it lead to the best kept-secret affair and possibly new found happiness, or does it lead to a broken family, unneeded stress, and public disgrace?

One sip. Does it lead to a fun uninhibited evening or does it lead to alcohol abuse, revoked privileges and possibly death?

One skipped day. Does it lead to a fun experience with friends or does it lead to dropping out of school?

One weekend splurging. Does it lead to a great weekend of fancy gadgets and clothing or does it lead to poor spending habits and inability to save for the future?

The answer is yes to both. That's the beauty of potential. We at least can go into our choices with our eyes completely wide open! No more surprises and false realities of "nothing will happen to me" lifestyles. Consider the potential of choice like ripple effects. How far do your ripples reach? For parents and others, how does the potential of your choice affect those closest to you? Your children? Family? Professional Peers? One you understand the potential of your choice, you can then begin to do the WORK of your choice.

THE WORK

This is where people in HabitLand make the biggest stumble AFTER making the choice, underestimating the work required! We see it all of the time. Someone quits their job. They stop going to gym. They pick the computer screen or affair over their mate with the assumption that the affair, poor health habits, dropping out, cutting corners is somehow "easier" than the alternative. News Flash…

The work is EXACTLY THE SAME NO MATTER WHAT YOU CHOOSE!

This time honored principle has never changed; not for the purpose or the person. Yet, in every generation, group, company or family there are those who will continually seek ways around it. HabitLanders particularly want is the easiest route! ANYTHING other than the work before us seems like a better choice. Struggling in school? Of course it looks easier to drop out. Going through a rough patch in your marriage? Sure. Make a call or download an app and "just see".

The work required to drop out of school, find a job or hustle without skills, and provide for self is the same work as one who doesn't drop out, miss a meal or two to get through, sacrifice 4-10 yrs. of their life for an education or future as a doctor, lawyer or whatever they choose.

The work required to yell back at the boss, get fired, find new employment, just to be able to say "Nobody talks to me like that!" is the same work required to remain quiet and humble, mindful than what is being said to you doesn't define you, and advance at your current job is the same type of work.

The work required to have an affair, learn someone new, seperate from family, manage the kids, pay child support and/or alimony is the same work as sticking it out, finding the right counselors, creating your safe and healthy space within your union. Barring abuse, the work is the same and if you're seeking a way out of HabitLand, then you gotta be in it to WORK!

ADVANCE & CONQUER

We discussed earlier the 3 Responses victims have to Fear, Change and Crisis. Now let's discuss the ONE response that actually works! "Advance and Conquer" (A&C) is the best response, but it's not easy! A&C requires:

- a unique sense of energy;

- a mindset and willingness to learn new skills along with the ability to master them with massive action;

- accepting that the event of crisis, change, and/or fear HAS HAPPENED and it didn't just happen to you – it happened to others as well; and,

- that this change, fear, or crisis represents an OPPORTUNITY!

My desire for change required something "new". I had seen my father and grandfather in Alcoholic Anonymous meetings for most of my teenage years... and I HATED IT! Statistically that setting for change only works for about 20% of addicts; and I wasn't any different. I needed tools beyond 12 steps. And therapists were no different for me. Nothing against the profession, but after 3 different therapists none of them could "relate" to me. They were older white men, married and apparently doing great in their marriage, and most importantly, they had no experience in my life!

I remember asking, "Have you ever cheated on your wife or done the things I'm here to get help with?" " No." he answered. Everything after that just fell on deaf ears. It was bad enough I felt horrible about all I had done but I couldn't even find someone who had made it out! Even though I was financially destitute, I got in contact with Craig Perra (my coach and now mentor and brother) and found the money!

What I remember that was most impactful and scary, was our first conversation. After a transparent conversation about our pasts, I told him how porn, sex, drugs and low self-esteem were destroying my life, but I didn't think I would be "cured" of it. I remember my grandfather said "I just want to know how to drink less!" That's what I wanted. And I told Craig as much. His response? "I don't do 'half-healed.' I only know full recovery so you can have a great life for your family. Let me know when you're ready." For the first time, I felt real fear! I was faced with the prospect of being without my addictions! My comfort. My victimhood and pass to HabitLand.

I learned so many lessons and discovered so much about myself within a 4-5 month period! I learned what exactly a habit is and how it related to addictions. How to change the thought to impact my actions and how to line it up with my cravings. How to communicate and LISTEN to myself and, most importantly, how to turn the parts of my life that weighed me down with guilt and shame into an opportunity of growth! None of which was easy! But like I said in the intro, this wasn't a pillow fight! For the first time in a healthy way...

I GOT SELFISH!

Selfish is a one of those words that immediately screams negativity! In fact, selfish behavior is considered almost immoral depending on the source. Especially when an addiction is present. All the actions of my past were compulsive, destructive, and of course selfish! I'm sure there are those who are reading this book and wondering, "Why not do it for your wife and kids? To save your career?" You see, it didn't matter what happened to my career and family if I didn't secure me first! If you have been on a plane, what instructions does the flight attendant always give? "In the event of an emergency and the air masks are lowered, SECURE YOURSELF FIRST, then others." Why? Because the pressure (lack of or strength of)will kill you before you can help another. Same applies in life.

Still don't believe you can be selfish? Selfless is the way to go? Great. On your next check cash it, divide it into 10 equal parts and give out nine to nine random people. Still think selfless is great? The truth is that we all only "give selflessly" to the extent that it won't impact us significantly. It sounds good to say "I'm selfless", but it's just a pretty way of saying your selfish, but just not that much.

There is a such thing as healthy selfish. Don't believe selfish is good? Ok. No matter how you look at it there is no benefit to you, your family or profession in any measure if you are somehow lesser. More importantly, if what you set as the motivation for your change is gone, then what's your reason to change now? Exactly. It takes some work to rewire the brain for this but HEALTHY SELFISH DOES EXIST! Next step...

I FOUND MY IDENTITY

Earlier in Part 1 we discussed how labels, roles and common trends craft our identity within HabitLand. When everything came to a head, I had no idea who I was! Everything I thought I was seemed fake or false or incomplete. No longer a husband or parent in the traditional sense. The success I gained from work seemed like a distant memory after being demoted twice. It was hard. What I learned is that there are essentially two parts to shaping your identity: Who you are when living in oblivion and who you are when seeking absolution.

Seeking Absolution

One of the challenges you'll face in remaking your identity as you make your Exodus from HabitLand is how people perceive and receive you. Just because you made your escape doesn't mean all is forgiven and forgotten. Most people try to seek amends, which I highly recommend. But what do you do if you aren't forgiven? You have to learn how to forgive YOURSELF! And that's where the Shit List comes in!

SHIT LIST!

We all got it. That thing or event from our past that we want to forget. The time(s) you were at your worst. One of the first tools I learned in developing my identity was to create a Shit List. I took everything that gave me the most shame and guilt and put it on a list! I had to separate the circumstances and outcomes of my life from who I truly was. In doing so, I identified what had to change to rid myself of the victim mindset.

This might just be the hardest part of our Exodus, but hang in there with me! Take some time and begin listing everything you hate about your life or what you've done. Try to list at least 4-5 things. Get started by finishing this sentence to come up with your shit list:

My life sucks because

1. _____

2. _____

3. _____

4. _____

5. _____

If you have more than 5 things feel free to use an additional sheet of paper. Once you have finished writing your Shit List, take a minute to process it. Own your shit and be <u>accountable</u> for your own unhappiness! Remember victims blame OTHERS for their unhappiness. In Exodus of HabitLand, you can't do shit about your unhappiness if it's another person's responsibility! Own your unhappiness if you want to change it!

Now, as fucked up as your list might be, look at your Shit List from another perspective and ask yourself these questions:

- How can you use this list to your advantage?
- How can you use it as a source of strength?

This simple change in perspective can turn your life from reactive to proactive. Once you see that you are responsible for your failures, then you can see that you are responsible for your successes. We all make mistakes and bad things happen, but the important question is: Can I use this failure or negativity to see what I don't want, and instead create what I do want?

Remember: Shit List = Opportunity for Growth

Part of my Shit List included having a double life. And not only that I lived a double life, but that my family got about, at most, 50% of my full worth. The opportunity? Well, everything I have acquired and lost: money, property, family; I got on *only* 50% of me. Good or bad, it wasn't even my full potential in any given direction. The real opportunity is "What does 100% of George in one direction look like?"

Another was my history of addiction and hiding. I knew that shame. It hurt, but I knew it. And when I could see the slightest glimpses within my children, my opportunity was that I didn't have to run from the conversation. I never had a talk with my dad about his addiction. He never shared the pits and falls and the works needed to rebuild. I share that with my children now. And in doing so ridding them of shame as well. It was evident when my youngest son was asked in school "What does your dad do for a living? To which he replied "My dad is a coach who helps people with addictions because that's what he had to deal with." and moved right into the next matter. All without a drip of shame.

Use the Shit List that you just created and turn each item from a negative into an opportunity. For each failure listed above, finish the following sentence:

I see an opportunity of growth when _____

Now, it was about these triggers representing an opportunity! My addictions; the very thing that cost me so much money became my profession, helping men across the globe. My health (sickle cell, poor diet, surgery, stroke) became the opportunity to develop my body in nontraditional ways, and also became a way to bond with my son. I now had boundless opportunities all around me!

Living In Oblivion

After dealing with the Shit List, Victor Bell of the Champion Army taught me about Living In Oblivion. Last man on Earth type of stuff.

"Close your eyes. Picture yourself in a restaurant, eating your favorite meal with everything you love. Your mom, sons, daughter, wife, siblings, and your career. Even your addictions! Take all the shit that gave you a label, role or purpose. Can you see them?"

"Yes."

"Cool. BANG! They're all gone. Dead. Now who are you?"

I was speechless. I couldn't think of an answer. It was the first time I had to see myself "naked". In my toil and work, I learned that I am powerful. Not He-Man or Superman powerful, but powerful enough to live the life I had lived and still be alive. I knew of others personally who died behind their addictions. I learned that I had more value than what I had credited myself for. My impact was more than others. I learned that I was born to be a weapon for God, and that He used my voice for such a output of His weapon. I learned that I was tolerant of more pain than I thought! I had been so used to being inebriated, high or otherwise numb that when sobriety actually came, I handled more pain better than when I was high. Still not quite complete, but armed with new opportunities from my Shit List as well as what I learned about myself in Oblivion, my identity at this point trumped my identity at any point in my life.

CRAVINGS

Back to the CRAVINGS! You should remember this from the Habit Cycle - The driving force behind the habit. So if we gonna have healthy habits, let's discuss the healthy cravings! Before my Exodus, my cravings were all surface! Sex, Drugs and Rock & Roll! Ok. No Rock & Roll, but you get my point.

Like most people, I thought my surface wants were my cravings/unmet needs! So, of course, I thought I "needed" to be high. I believed I "craved" sex. I accepted that I had an "unmet need" to have control and authority in all situations. The truth was, that was the only way I knew to satisfy my craving.

But I was wrong. You see, I translated my REAL cravings into coping addictions. And like most addicts and those who have never HEALTHILY satisfied their cravings; the high, buzz and thrill of the moment NEVER LASTED! And just like every other addict, I was left chasing that first high that brought me the closest to what I thought was my cravings.

So if my cravings weren't about sex, porn, and drugs -- then what were they?

Legacy.

Relevance.

Significance.

Pay back for everything I'm owed.

Whether I was a social services practitioner, teacher, salesman, porn addict, drug abuser, and now an Addictions Coach and Habit Trainer, these cravings lied at the center of all of these ventures and exploits. If I helped a child and/or his family, that gave me significance, relevance, and a legacy. When I came home and see my wife covered in food from cooking, baby mess, and tired, I felt like I wasn't relevant, significant. I didn't feel like I had something worth leaving behind. No legacy. So I resorted to porn and affairs. Hell, even when I spent money that I didn't have, and money my family needed on drugs or women, I somehow felt that I was "getting back what I was owed" from the lack of affection, attention, and whatever else I felt I did without!

Now my legacy was more about what I am remembered for, rather than being remembered. Significance and Relevance was more about what I contributed rater than what others thought of me. And I learned that the feeling of being owed was more about how I valued myself rather than how others valued me.

As we go forward, remember, just as surely as we need food, water, and shelter to physically survive, we MUST satisfy our emotional and psychological needs as well. The longer they go unmet, the longer your sub and addictions will spiral further into destructive and harmful habits, however they may manifest in your life!

GOALS:
WHAT - HOW - WHY

I used to absolutely suck in making goals! In hindsight the majority of the goals I pursued were the goals of my parents ambition or my method of rebellion. Now don't get me or my parents wrong. They weren't the pushy type. But the did set a standard. And like most parents, they pushed for their children to meet and exceed. I think it's hard for most parents to allow their children to to really discover who they naturally are and what they're naturally talented in. It's human nature to think you know what's best for another.

What I find most intriguing about goals is how they have increased for some groups and limited for others. Today women and children are told to literally be anything they want! To pursue it with passion and authority! To which I commend and whole-heartedly support. However, men on the other hand have been placed in this "go to school - get a good job - SETTLE DOWN - get married - have a family - retire - DIE" script. This fits for some. Not for addicts. Not for entrepreneurs and high level business men. Not for police officers and firefighters. Not for men seeking more engagement than a cubicle, emails and water cooler conversations. These men like myself needed MORE! And once I found my healthy selfish and my identity, I learned how to make real goals.

WHAT

Most of us make goals for the day, month or maybe the year. The easy goals. These were the small and surface goals that no longer fueled me! Addicts, Fighters, Entrepreneurs and high-level executives and men of the like we need more to go for; something more passionate and rewarding than the addictions or lifestyle we seek to change. Whether or not I could achieve it wasn't really the question. The goal had to be large enough, yet realistic enough for me to pursue it. After all, the point of coming out of HabitLand isn't to live a dull life WITHOUT your vices; it's to have a life SUPERIOR to your vices! Let's take money for example. Let's say the previous goal was to make an extra $5,000. Make it $50,000. If it's to pay rent for the year, make it to buy a house within 5 years. Make the goal worthy of your best life possible!

Your goals should be reflective of what you want in the most healthy way, not what you need. The only reason for a small goal is to hit a smaller target. Now there is nothing wrong with this thinking, it just doesn't belong with the actual goal! Make the goal and own it!

HOW

This is the tricky part to creating goals… HOW DO YOU ACCOMPLISH IT? There has to be thousands of books on this as well as countless speakers on the topic, but a few things remain consistent with each iteration of how to achieve a goal.

Just Do It

Quite possibly the most cliche thing to ever say, but this is where the magic begins! Just do. You'll make mistakes. Just do. You'll lose money before making tons of money. Just do. The beauty of just do is that you'll find yourself around others who just do. Just like victims find victims, doers will find doers. And you'll learn everything you'll need from that group and the next and the next. Just do!

Before Nike, there was Art Williams, Founder of Primerica. He had a famous speech titled "Just Do It". This excerpt explains the "how":

> **"What does the \$500K a year person do, the \$50K person doesn't do? You look outside and study those two individuals, everything seems to be the same. They're both of the same sex, they're both of the same age, they have the same training, the same positions, the same contract, the same friends, benefits, both are successful, they work hard, they're good family people, make tough commitments. But what's the difference? He pays the price a little bit more, he works hard a little bit more…."**

> **"If you wanna become someone, do it. If you wanna go into business, do it. If you wanna become financially independent, do it. I hear too much talkin'…"**

> **"Art, Art what's the primary difference between winners and losers? The winners do it…. They do it, and do it, and do it, and do it, until the job gets done. And then they talk about how great it is to finally have achieved something UNIQUE."**

Micro-Habits

So how do you eat an elephant? That's right… ONE BITE AT A TIME! You've learned micro-habits your entire life. Your formal education is based on micro-habits. Bits of information all to culminate in a diploma or a degree. Yet, it's the one thing we all of a sudden forget when we are trying to achieve something monumental. It's why we start out with a goal making the "what" small; not realizing we just made the micro-habit the main goal! As I battled my addictions, I found that by using micro-habits, I achieved success at a greater rate than attempting the big habit change all at once.

So what is a micro-habit? Micro-habit or "mini habit" is "a very small positive behavior that you force yourself to do every day; it's 'too small to fail' nature makes it weightless, deceptively powerful, and a superior habit building strategy. You will have no choice but to believe in yourself when you're always moving forward. The barrier to the first step is so low that even depressed or 'stuck' people can find early success and begin to reverse their lives right away." Stephen Guise, <u>Mini-Habits: Smaller Habits, Bigger Results (2013)</u>.

Take for example the guy who wants to lose weight. He wants a habit of good eating 24 hours a day, 7 days a week. He wants to go to the gym 5 times a week and run 2 miles a day! Sounds like a great habit huh? The problem is that this brother more than likely has never engaged in such activities and lifestyle change. It's a literal shock to the system and a massive set up for failure!!

Instead of eating good every day, we begin to have at least one meal per day that meets the diet requirement. Instead of going to the gym 5 times a week and running 2 miles per day, we first start with daily, bi-weekly, weekly or even monthly walks around the block! Micro habits allow us to begin slightly outside of our comfort zones and experience success in the process. Is walking the block physically equivalent to a 2-mile run? No. But it trumps sitting on the couch doing nothing, and it builds you into the habit you desire.

I've always wanted a pretty close family, siblings and all. The kind of family that stayed in contact all the time! Well, I don't have that, at least not at first or in my Exodus. If the big habit was family functions, get-togethers, and sharing joyful moments with people that don't even talk to each other, what was going to be the micro habit?

I simply started texting them, every day! LOL. Nothing big. Just some genuine words that I wanted to share. What was the result? I started getting text messages back! Not surface stuff, but real communication! My sister, who I almost never spoke with once our lives began growing, started texting me back! My other sister became more and more comfortable asking me "big brother" questions! My dad was appreciative! My daughter and sons would try to beat me to the punch and text me first! And then they decided to get comfortable with it! The first time I forgot to text them in the morning, my mother was all over me! "So you just not going to wish me well today? Did I do something? You back to the 'old' George?"

Do we all get together today and share in each other's life? No. My parents are divorced, and my sisters can't stand each other. But before we can do that and create that habit, we just had to engage one another. Value one another. Or at least see that someone was willing to make the first step.

I simply asked myself, "What is the smallest thing I can do to impact this area of my life?" Not a call. I didn't write letters. No random surprise visits. Just a few keystrokes on my phone has placed us closer than before, which also means we are one step closer to that sense of family I desire.

Keystone Habits

Alright. So if you eat an elephant one bite at a time, how do you *remind* yourself to eat the elephant? How many times have you started something, thinking it would only have an effect in a particular area, just to find that it gives an effect in a totally different area? Like when you started a new workout routine to lose weight and tone up, and find you're more productive at work? Or maybe when you went to bed earlier to get to work on time, and the intimacy between you and your spouse increased or was able to spend more quality time with your closest bonds. You found a keystone habit!

Keystone habits say that success doesn't depend on getting every single thing right, but instead relies on identifying a few key priorities and fashioning them into powerful levers.

I learned of two significant keystone habits that fed my addictions and my creation of healthy habits. The first was hygiene. Now admittedly, I'm a bit of a hygiene fanatic! My family can attest. I'll spend almost an hour showering with the best "antibacterial" soap, loofah, facial cleanser, etc. You name it, I used it. But at the height of my addiction, I didn't care. I felt bad and smelled bad. But here's what I learned about my hygiene as a keystone habit. The nights I didn't wash I was almost 100% guaranteed to indulge in my addictions! When I washed, a significant drop in acting out manifested.

Another keystone habit that aided in creating healthy habits was working out. And not just working out, but working out with my son. While the workout was initially designed for him to lose weight and for me to gain weight, the outcome was that we grew significantly closer, allowing for more in-depth conversations and communication. Quite possibly the most unexpected outcome from working out.

WHY

This is probably the most important part of you making a goal - WHY you make the goal! In short, your why is the default when the "feelings" to do so start to dissipate. The problem most of us run into is that we don't create a sufficient "WHY". I, like most of my clients, had our why rooted in another person or external source. We wanted a relationship to make parents proud. Finances to please wife and kids. A body to be admired by others. We can't win that way. Remember, we are in HEALTHY selfish mode now!

Assume a financial goal. Most would state for the why that "I want to provide for my kids." I want to take my wife on a cruise and shopping spree." "I want to be debt-free." All of those sound good, but none of them are the real why. The real why is "I want financial freedom!" If you live in the best school district, you don't really care about putting your child in the best private school. Your wife may never want a trip around the world and heaven forbid if you actually learn financial principles to become debt-free. Then your "Why" is non existent.

It's not that your family, career, outward objects can not be the goal, but if you can't articulate what that goal or why does for you, then frankly you're fucked. Your Why needs to satisfy YOU, not another's!

I GOT SOME KICK ASS TOOLS!

I don't care who you are, at some point the motivation doesn't work. You just can't be "pumped up" to get out of every rut. Make it literal. If you were stranded on the side of the road with a flat, what would get the tire fixed, a pep talk or someone cheering you on or some damn tools to get your ass out? Exactly. And more importantly, you need the RIGHT TOOLS! Do you want to change a tire with a thousand screwdrivers OR one good jack and lug wrench? EXACTLY! So let's get you some working tools!

KICK ASS TOOL NO. 1:

Mindfulness

One of the first tools I adopted was Mindfulness. Mindfulness by definition is practically the opposite of a habit. While a habit is "the automatic reaction to external stimuli," Mindfulness is "being present, at the moment, on purpose, and most importantly, WITHOUT JUDGMENT"! Short version is the exact opposite of a habit! You ever hear how someone quits smoking and their senses hit overdrive? Scents and smells get stronger and more intense? Well, that's what life became! When I began practicing mindfulness and viewing life without judgment, I became aware of what was happening around me. Life wasn't automatic anymore. No more autopilot and crashing in HabitLand.

What started off as daily meditation for a few seconds a day (seriously, in the beginning I couldn't keep my eyes closed longer than 30 secs. And that was at a great strain!), soon grew to minutes and hours of mindfulness. Yes MINDFULNESS, not meditation! It allowed me to have a greater understanding of my body, my relationships, my actions. The best part of mindfulness was me not being invested in the "feelings". No judgement! No right, wrong, good or bad. Whatever it was it was and all I can do is plan best from this point forward. No regrets or lofty expectations.

I discovered things as little as source of body pains or why I was always 5-10 minutes late for getting my son from school to major things like becoming a better driver, and actually listening to others when communicated to. However, the biggest thing that manifested from Mindfulness was full awareness of my triggers! Remember from the introduction; the habit cycle is trigger - thought - action.

Here's the biggest takeaway for mindfulness. It releases the shame and guilt of the past and of my triggers. And once the shame and guilt was gone, I could make a real plan of action.

KICK ASS TOOL NO. 2:

First Thought WRONG - 2nd Thought RIGHT

Now it's time for precision aim! People around the globe ridiculously mess up creating and breaking habits by focusing on the wrong parts. Aim to attack those Deadly Thoughts from Part 1. Some people attack the triggers, just to be met with the frustration of never fully escaping them. Others attack the action. That provides a modicum of success, but it's never long standing. The only place we can make AND sustain the change is, to begin with the thoughts! Specifically, AT ITS INFANCY!

We cause exponentially more harm than good when we hold on to thoughts and the energy they carry throughout the day. They linger and grow. How often had you had the anticipating thought of a good meal, a great date or encounter. The anticipation builds throughout the day causing the expression of happiness, joy and elation for the encounter or moment. Now flip it and think about those deadly thoughts you let fester and grow. They don't become easier to manage. If anything, they already shifted your thinking and actions towards it, more than likely resulting in a behavior you didn't want to engage in. More importantly, that energy is wasted!

So we attack our thoughts as soon as mindfully possible! Once we identify the thought we attack with our new tool in the "space" right after the wrong thought and before the action. To keep myself aware, I approach most if not ALL of my thoughts assuming they are wrong! Whether you're an addict or former addict like myself, or simply been unaware of your thought patterns, the majority of our first thoughts are wrong!

- "I should hit the snooze button and get an extra 10 minutes of sleep." **WRONG!**

- "My spouse won't find out if I sleep with this person." **WRONG!**

- "I'm sore. I can quit my workout now and nobody would know." **WRONG!**

- "I absolutely SUCK in math!" **WRONG!**

- "I should give that guy the finger for cutting me off!" **WRONG!**

You get it by now. All those little thoughts you had that you felt had little meaning and supported your comfort, wrong thoughts! The problem is that we often justify our thoughts based on severity of consequences, the Triple E's, or because we know it will lead to behavior we seek to change. To create habit change, it's imperative we change our thoughts to the next best option! In fact, say it outloud if you can to really solidify it.

So let's replay with the 2nd Thought RIGHT!

- "I should hit the snooze button and get an extra 10 minutes of sleep." **WRONG!**
- "It's about time this alarm went off! LET'S GET TO WORK!" **RIGHT!!**
- "My spouse won't find out if I sleep with this person." **WRONG!**
- "I have the best spouse in the world. I can't wait to see them." **RIGHT!!**
- "I'm sore. I can quit now, and nobody would know." **WRONG!**
- "I made a commitment to myself to get better and NOT QUIT!" **RIGHT!!**
- "I absolutely SUCK in math!" **WRONG!**
- "I need more practice in math, but I can do this!" **RIGHT!!**

You've done it before. Like that time you would do something but you THOUGHT of the consequence and decided against it. We've all done it before. Now let's see how it works when we don't wait for the worst consequence to avoid. After doing the activity showing the actions that happen AFTER the deadly 1st thought, it's pretty easy to see how the action changes with the healthy 2nd thought. Here's the greatest benefit to creating the second thought: you create a CHOICE! Remember, choice is POWER. Before, you operated by the first thought! Now you have a CHOICE between the first AND the second!

KICK ASS TOOL NO. 3:

Trigger Response Plan (TRP)

Now that I was aware of my triggers, you know that feeling after you learn something? That feeling like you just got the keys to the city? Hit the lotto? That's how I felt after learning 1st Thought WRONG - 2nd Thought RIGHT! I was like, "Oh yeah! I know how to beat my habits!" Yeah… WRONG!

What I learned shortly after was that triggers ESCALATE! You got your small triggers like a bill collector call (don't act like it's just me) and you got BIG triggers like death, loss, around drugs and/or wrong peers, etc. The big triggers are going to require an ACTION plan to get past them successfully. If I had a bad day at work I could do 1st Thought WRONG - 2nd Thought RIGHT all day, but if I had an argument with my wife, I needed a plan to move forward or the deadly thoughts, no matter how many right thoughts I used, would overwhelm me.

I needed more than a right thought. And odds are you do too! When I learned this lesson, it was like, "If plan A doesn't work, I can use plans B - Z all at one time!"

Bottom line: You ARE going to be triggered, and you ARE going to have WRONG thoughts. Therefore, you need a plan to help you embrace your power of choice - a plan that becomes a habit - a plan to create space between thought and action.

So what exactly is a TRP?

TRP is a series of three - five activities that you can perform within two minutes just about anywhere that will help you transmute the energy used for the habit of change and harmful thoughts away from compulsivity towards creating a great life.

Step 1: *MAKE THE FIRST STOP IN THE PROCESS*

- 1st Thought Wrong - 2nd Thought Right (MANDATORY).

Steps 2 - 4: *LEAVE FANTASY AND RETURN TO REALITY BY GETTING PHYSICAL*

- Snap Back to Reality: sharp "pop" or snap causing an immediate energy shift (wristbands, rubber bands, bracelets, etc.)
- Mindful breathing: 3 - 7 breaths while you direct all of your attention to counting breaths, to the exclusion of all else.
- Mindful Activity: Jumping jacks, walk, push-ups that are done slow and mindfully ensuring that you focus only on your breathing, counting, and muscle strain and pull.

Step 5: *HEALTHY VERBAL AND EMOTIONAL CONNECTION*

- Call Someone! A friend, relative, mtg, group call, etc.
- Don't have to talk to this person about your habits
- Safe space to communicate to change the habit of change energy

What we're doing here is combining the power of mindfulness with habits. Essentially, you are using the trigger response plan to hack your habit cycle, create space, and embrace your power of choice.

This was the power I needed to handle my triggers! Remember, triggers are biologically hardwired. They don't go away. And for me, I thought every damn trigger was just a sign of how messed up I was or how everything and everyone was against me!

To use this tool SUCCESSFULLY, you need to remember three important things before you go and apply it:

1. This, nor anything else, will NOT make you stop the behavior; it's designed for you to be able to make a CHOICE to do the right thing.

2. Don't limit the TRP to only one area of your life. Take every opportunity to create multiple TRP's for various areas of your life! If you exhibit any behavior in any area of your life, do the TRP.

3. You need new TRPs for new levels of life. You need to understand that the TRP you create today, may not be effective for the triggers you encounter a year later. In the words of Meek Mill, "There's levels to this!" If you expect growth, you have to expect new triggers. The middle class doesn't have the same problems as the lower class, and accordingly, the upper 10% don't share the problems of the 90%, but they have triggers nonetheless.

I remember when I decided to start my coaching practice. I found myself at home, in front of a computer with a lot of time on my hands! The TRP I had when I was doing door-to-door sales 10 hours a day for 6-7 days a week lost its effect in this new phase of life. I had to kick it up a notch!

Tweak your TRP's needed and make it work for YOU! Write down your trigger response plan in your phone or on a piece of paper that you keep in your pocket so that you can reference it whenever necessary. You will use this plan throughout the rest of your life.

Once you have a plan and you know what to do, you will feel that you have more control. Once you understand that you have control, you can create more space and truly begin to embrace your power of choice.

THE TAKEAWAY

Habits are difficult to understand, let alone make or break, especially when trying to understand how they work in and around our lives. But they are needed; and like most good things, they can be abused and manipulated to cause harm. So before we move into HabitLand, review the following takeaways from the habit cycle and definition that you can readily refer to!

ROCK BOTTOM

- Great place for a new start
- Brings clarity
- Inspires creativity

CHOICES

- 5th Step of the Habit Cycle
- Equals Power
- Potential of choice is greater than "right now"
- Regardless of what choice you make, the same amount of work is required

ADVANCE & CONQUER REQUIRES:

- A unique sense of energy;
- A mindset and willingness to learn new skills along with the ability to master them with massive action;
- Accepting that the event of crisis, change, and/or fear HAS HAPPENED didn't just happen to you and that it happened to others as well; and,
- That this change, fear, or crisis represents an OPPORTUNITY!

IDENTITY

- Who you are when what you know isn't around you
- Who you are when you are not forgiven of your past
- Is found with the shit of our past, but is not the ACTIONS or OUTCOME of our past

CRAVINGS

- The why behind the feeling of the action
- The cravings don't change, but there is a HEALTHY alternative

I GOT SELFISH!

- A lesser you never benefited the ones we love
- Healthy Selfish benefits those closest to you

GOALS: THE WHAT - HOW - WHY

What

- MUST be as bigger than "average"
- Provides as much, if not greater passion, as the source of addiction

How

- Just Do It
- Create micro habits around larger goals
- Create keystone habits to remind you to engage in the goal or micro habit

Why

- Must be about you, not another

3 KICK ASS TOOLS!

- Mindfulness
- 1st Thought WRONG/2nd Thought RIGHT
- Trigger Response Plan

HABITLAND
CONCLUSION

So what have you learned about HabitLand? First and foremost, I just hope you realize that HabitLand is real. It does exist within every segmented population that exists. HabitLand doesn't discriminate along any lines that currently divide our society. Secondly, I hope you learned that both our good and bad habits reside in HabitLand. Yes, we do need it. For everything? No. But we do need it.

Our job is to be mindful enough to recognize when our thoughts, distractions, and responses are in need, and make the change -- IN THE MOMENT!

Ideally you also gained a greater understanding of how and why addicts operate the way they do as well as the knowledge to empower yourself or another to their Exodus of HabitLand. You should know that this is a lifetime of work in controlling your thoughts to change your habits and satisfy your cravings in the most healthy way possible. But it's worth it! The daily fight needed to regain your identity, position yourself, family, and business for success is more than worth the fight involved.

This isn't easy. I still struggle daily with my Triple E's! Every now and then, my deadly thoughts arise. However, who I am without those anchors in my life is truly greater than any version of myself prior.

The same exists for you! Young or old. Scattered in direction or committed to a path. Male or female. Black, white or anything else. As much as HabitLand doesn't discriminate, neither does the option of a great life. Exodus from HabitLand doesn't mean an Exodus from your problems, but it does mean you start asking the right questions in those moments. It means you'll lose your "Whoa is ME!" default to a "Who am I IN THIS MOMENT?" and let that define your next course.

So if you're reading this, you still have time! Stop wasting it and make the Exodus out of your HABITLAND!